Still Life

T0290792

Charles Way was born and raised in Crediton, Devon. He trained as an actor at the Rose Bruford College in London then joined Leeds Playhouse theatre for whom he wrote his first professional play in 1978. He has since written over forty plays, many for young people, which have been produced all over the world.

Charles specialises in the use of fairytale and myth to create pieces for the modern world. *Red Red Shoes* was a great success at the Royal Opera House in May 2004, winning the Children's Award from the Arts Council of England.

He is currently working with the Sechuan People's Theatre in Chengdu, China, on a play inspired by Pericles which will be performed in China and at the West Yorkshire Playhouse.

Charles has recently directed his own adaptation of the Icelandic novel *Independent People* by Halldor Laxness, which toured England with New Perspective Theatre, then went to Iceland.

Charles has spent most of his creative life in Wales and has worked with many Welsh companies. His plays there include *On The Black Hill* (Made in Wales), *Ill Met By Moonlight* and *In The Bleak Midwinter* (Hijinx Theatre), *The Tinderbox* (Gwent Theatre) and *A Spell Of Cold Weather* (Sherman Theatre), which won the Writers' Guild award for Best Children's Play.

In 2004 he was commissioned by 'Imagination Stage' in Washington, USA to write *Merlin and the Cave of Dreams*, and this has been nominated for a Helen Hayes award for Outstanding New Play.

Charles is a member of the Writers' Guild of Great Britain and the Welsh Academy.

Also by Charles Way

A Spell of Cold Weather
In the Bleak Midwinter
Looking Out to See
The Classic Fairy Tales Retold for the Stage
The Flood
The Search for Odysseus
Three Plays
Three Plays for Young People

Still Life

Charles Way

DRUM THEATRE PLYMOUTH
www.theatreroyal.com

 Creative Partnerships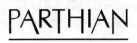

PARTHIAN

Parthian
The Old Surgery
Napier Street
Cardigan
SA43 1ED

www.parthianbooks.co.uk

First published in 2005
© Charles Way 2005
All Rights Reserved

ISBN 1-902638-66-2

Printed and bound by Dinefwr Press, Llandybïe, Wales
Typeset by type@lloydrobson.com & Parthian

Cover design: Lucy Llewellyn
Cover image: Dragonfly Design

Parthian is an independent publisher which works with
the support of the Arts Council of Wales and the Welsh
Books Council

British Library Cataloguing in Publication Data – A
cataloguing record for this book is available from the
British Library

Theatre of Science

The Theatre Royal Plymouth's *Theatre Of Science* is an exciting new initiative for Plymouth and the wider region, bringing theatre and science together in innovative and creative ways. It also hopes to create a lasting legacy of science-based plays for British theatre in general.

Key elements of the year-long project are three specially commissioned theatre productions; scientists-in-residence working alongside theatre practitioners; an exciting new science drama programme for local schools and partner community groups; and an intensive programme of public projects and events. Participants of all ages and abilities have the opportunity to be involved.

Particular issues to be addressed include biomedical science and the ethical and moral issues behind disease immunity, eugenics, the ageing process and contemporary genomics. This unique project explores the potential for performance arts not only to promote an understanding of contemporary biomedical science, but also to establish a dialogue between the often conflicting cultures of theatre and science.

Theatre Of Science has three aims:
- to research, test and evaluate innovative ways of bringing dramatists and scientists together to shape medical-linked theatre, community and education projects;
- to use the performing arts to address the major scientific, ethical and moral problems and opportunities of biomedicine in the 21st century;
- to enable creative science partnerships which inspire and develop new audiences and future practitioners for both science and theatre.

Theatre of Science presents three specially-commissioned productions – two in the Drum Theatre and one at TR2. Each production has an extensive education programme for local schools.

The first *Theatre of Science* production was *Seeing Without Light* by Simon Turley (Drum Theatre, Thursday 27 January – Saturday 5 February 2005). This play was originally developed in association with Dr Jane McHarg, Research Fellow at the Peninsula Medical School, and Dr Penny Fidler at @Bristol. The play explores the ramifications of the discovery of genetic immunity to HIV, attitudes to the disease in its African context and the similar responsibilities of scientists and artists to their work. This is a contemporary drama that questions universal themes of love, life and death in the 21st century, while exploring how life, art and science imitate one another. The Eddystone Trust in Plymouth was the community partner for this play and eleven local schools worked with science and theatre practitioners on workshops exploring the biomedical and ethical issues of HIV research and treatment. They presented their own plays at TR2 in January 2005, before the first production of *Seeing Without Light*.

The second play is *Still Life* by Charles Way (Drum Theatre, Thursday 14 – Saturday 23 April 2005). This play explores the link between DNA and longevity and the ethics of genetic research and how science is challenging not only our moral universe but what it is that makes us human. Six local schools have engaged with issues surrounding genetic research and its implications, and will perform their resulting plays at TR2 in May 2005. The Nomony Centre is the community partner for this play. Dr John Spicer at the University of Plymouth, and Dr Penny Fidler at @Bristol have advised on and supported this production.

Special by Peter Morgan completes the trilogy of plays and explores the medical and cultural history of eugenics and its contemporary resonances with modern genomics.

This play benefited from a Wellcome-funded script development week at the Theatre Royal in 2003 and subsequent research at the Wellcome Library. The play received its first reading at RADA in April 2004 and a second in Sweden over the summer as part of a Wellcome Trust initiative.

The *Theatre of Science*'s SciArt laboratory offers a chance for artists locally and all over the country to work in collaboration with scientists on new ideas. The SciArt lab offers a series of commissions to explore the links between art and science.

Rebecca Gould, Associate Director at Theatre Royal Plymouth, has worked closely with the Peninsula Medical School on *Theatre of Science* and the project has been generously funded by a grant from the Wellcome Trust and forms part of a collaborative programme with Creative Partnerships.

The author wishes to thank William Finkenrath, Rebecca Gould, Gary Meredith, Kate Saxon and Jeff Teare for their kind assistance with this text.

Still Life

First performed at the Drum Theatre Plymouth
14 April 2005.

Cast:

Charles (mid forties)	–	Malcolm James
Simon (early twenties)	–	Danny Nutt
Voice of the Mirror	–	Sarah Ball
Voice of Susan	–	Lisa Stevenson

Creative Team:

Director	–	Kate Saxon
Designer	–	Alex Eales
Lighting Designer	–	Bruno Poet
Video Designer	–	Thomas Hall
Sound Designer	–	Richard Price
Assistant Director	–	Alexander Ferris
Producer	–	Rebecca Gould
Production Manager	–	Nick Soper
Stage Manager	–	Annabel Ingram
Deputy Stage Manager	–	Claire Teesdale
Wardrobe Supervisor	–	Dina Hall
Wardrobe Mistress	–	Cheryl Hill
Consultant	–	Jeff Teare
Voice-over Sound Engineer	–	Ant Hales for Side UK
Scientific Advisors	–	Dr Penny Fidler
		Dr John Spicer

The audience enter a space which is, in effect, the house in which the play is set. The play happens around and among them. The space needs to have a simple beauty and its walls should be clear so images can be projected on to them. It is the house of an artist who has recently been working with stained glass.

In the opening scene, the mirror is a neon shape and when CHARLES speaks to the mirror and it replies (VOICE OVER) it becomes light.

The play is set in the future.

Act One

CHARLES: When I was little I painted my father's face.
I painted my father's face once a year
and the lines on his face
from shallow streams ran to deep ravines
a map of tribulations,
and when he died I painted
his cold diminished self
and my daughter wept at his strangeness,
and I painted her face.
And when she was old
I painted her face
and when she died
I painted her face
and fear tore the brush from my hand.
I ran into the woods, like a child
and hid my face, like a child.
I stepped into another story
and lived all the days of my life
in the leaves of this dark fairy tale.

Light shines through stained glass. CHARLES stands before a free-standing MIRROR. There is no glass in the frame so his image can be seen from every angle.

CHARLES: How do I look?

MIRROR: You look well.

CHARLES: I look the same?

MIRROR: The same as?

CHARLES: Yesterday.

MIRROR: Yes Charles.

CHARLES: A strange day.

MIRROR: It is. We're glad Charles, that this day has come. Glad for you – and we would like you to know, how grateful we are. The people you have helped would want you to know.

CHARLES: Heart rate?

MIRROR: Hundred and five.

CHARLES: I can't be calm.

MIRROR: It wouldn't be natural.

CHARLES: Has he left home yet?

MIRROR: Yes.

CHARLES: Is he safe?

MIRROR: We're taking great care.

CHARLES: You won't interfere.

MIRROR: As we discussed and agreed.

CHARLES: I don't want you to interfere.

MIRROR: Only if necessary, as we arranged. Be strong Charles, you are his best hope.

CHARLES paces.

CHARLES: I'd like to be at the gate to greet him.

MIRROR: You know that cannot be.

CHARLES: Surely today is different.

MIRROR: In most respects today is the same.

CHARLES: Let me go to the gate. It would seem odd not to – from his point of view. File the request.

Silence.

MIRROR: Your request has been denied.

CHARLES: This 'transfer' will not work – if I'm not given a free hand. He'll go insane.

MIRROR: If it does not work then you must remain here.

CHARLES: Thank you.

MIRROR: It's better to be clear.

CHARLES: As a mirror should be. (*He paces.*) Did he see anyone, this morning, before he left?

MIRROR: No.

CHARLES: Did he speak to anyone? Make any calls?

MIRROR: Yes.

CHARLES: To whom?

MIRROR: His partner.

CHARLES: I'd like to hear that conversation. File the request.

Silence.

MIRROR: Your request has been granted.

Phone rings, followed by conversation:

SUSAN: Hello?

SIMON: Hi sleepy head.

SUSAN: Hi, you're early.

SIMON: It's a big day. I just wanted to say hello, hear your voice...

SUSAN (*puts on a stupid voice*): Hello Simon, this is my voice.

SIMON: Nice.

Silence.

SUSAN: Are you alright?

SIMON: Yeah, yeah, just...

SUSAN: Nervous?

SIMON: Do I sound nervous?

SUSAN: You'll be fine.

SIMON: That nervous?

SUSAN: No. Yes.

They laugh.

SUSAN: You'll be fine once you're there. What time will I see you?

SIMON: Late – the guy's a recluse, lives way out of town in some secret location. They're sending a special transport to pick me up.

SUSAN: Who is?

SIMON: His people. He's a rich man – he has people.

SUSAN: Stay the night.

SIMON: With him?

SUSAN: No, not with him – with me, idiot.

SIMON: Of course...

SUSAN: Do well, be good, come home okay – I need to to talk to you.

SIMON: Oh?

SUSAN: Don't worry...

SIMON: What about?

SUSAN: I want to be face to face. Tonight, we'll talk tonight...

SIMON: Okay... cos...

SUSAN: What?

SIMON: I need to talk to you too...

SUSAN: Okay...

SIMON: No I mean... oh God, it's just, you know – we've moved so fast... and I love you so much I can hardly think straight...

SUSAN: We'll speak tonight.

SIMON: I do love you.

SUSAN: I know.

SIMON: Bye....

Silence. A sound. A light.

CHARLES: He's here?

MIRROR: He's at the gate.

CHARLES: Show me.

Image of SIMON waiting in front of a white wall. He looks up at the camera.

CHARLES: Poor boy.

SIMON: Hello, um, this is Simon from the New Arts Review. I've come to to talk to Charles, as arranged. Hello?

MIRROR: Welcome him.

CHARLES: Let him stay there, for one moment more.

SIMON: Hello, is anyone there? Hello?

MIRROR: Are you ready Charles?

CHARLES: Open the gate, and may God forgive us.

On Screen, behind SIMON, a dark square becomes apparent in the white wall, which SIMON now sees.

CHARLES: Come in Simon. Come in.

SIMON: Right.

On Screen, he walks into the dark square thus disappearing and emerging, physically, in the house.

SIMON: Hi. Hi. I'm Simon. Thanks for seeing me, it's a great honour.

CHARLES: It's nice to meet you.

SIMON offers his hand, CHARLES declines.

CHARLES: You'll forgive me, I'm not used to people. I don't mean to be rude, you are very welcome.

SIMON: Oh that's fine, no problem.

CHARLES: How was your journey?

SIMON: Good, I seem to have slept most of the way – don't know where I am.

CHARLES: I try to keep the whereabouts of this house a secret.

SIMON: The price of fame.

CHARLES: Precisely.

SIMON: This, um, shouldn't take too long. A few hours perhaps.

CHARLES: What's a few hours?

SIMON: I left my ID with your driver, and my phone.

CHARLES: That's fine.

SIMON: You know what it's like: can't move in the city without ID.

CHARLES: So I hear.

SIMON: Well it's a nice house, for staying in, if you have to.

CHARLES: You like it?

SIMON: I didn't know what to expect. The ID? And phone?

CHARLES: When you leave they will be returned.

SIMON: Well, we should make a start. You don't mind if I record the interview?

CHARLES: Everything here is recorded anyway, so I can send you a copy...

SIMON: How do you mean?

CHARLES: It's part of the house – it records what we say, do. Security.

SIMON: Oh.

CHARLES: In fact the house is rather splendid, and there are gardens, and rivers – I'll show you round.

SIMON: I'd like that. I'd rather use my own recording stuff if that's okay. (*He fumbles nervously with his recording equipment.*)

CHARLES: As you wish. You were born in Reykjavik?

SIMON: Yes?

CHARLES: Simon Gudmundsun.

SIMON: You've done some research?

CHARLES: Security.

SIMON: I moved to London when I was six.

CHARLES: Did you always want to be a journalist?

SIMON: No, I wanted to be an artist, I just lacked the happy accident of talent. Anyhow I don't consider myself to be a journalist, as such. I write about art, obviously; not news.

CHARLES: I understand, art is not news.

SIMON: Not unless it's stolen. So.

CHARLES: So.

SIMON: These machines: crap. Anyway I can't thank you enough for seeing me.

CHARLES: It's a pleasure, and a duty.

SIMON: No one believed me at first, at the office, that you'd asked to see me. I have to tell them why.

CHARLES: You were recommended.

SIMON: Oh? Who by?

CHARLES: Those who know your work.

SIMON: That's the bit I don't understand – no one knows my work, I'm unknown.

CHARLES: Not true. I've read some of your articles. They're young, fresh. As you get older you gather shadows, strange notions of what's good and bad in art, in life, in anything. You have the advantage of youth. You're shadowless, to a degree.

SIMON: I see, well I'm grateful in any case. I think they were about to fire me.

CHARLES: I doubt that.

SIMON: No it's true, this interview will boost my career. Big time.

CHARLES: Don't worry about your career, Simon. It only exists looking back.

SIMON: I don't know. (*Of his sound equipment:*) damn thing. For a young guy a career can only exist in the future. Right, I think it's working now....

CHARLES: You're married?

SIMON: No.

CHARLES: No?

SIMON: No. But I...

CHARLES: Have someone?

SIMON: Yeah, well we all need someone.

Silence.

CHARLES: That's true.

SIMON: You live alone here?

CHARLES: Yes, but not today.

SIMON: I can't imagine that – living alone. I mean really alone.

CHARLES: I have my work.

SIMON: Indeed. What I thought we could do is look at certain works of art... in your book – it's magnificent... and talk about the progression, how it evolved, over the years. It would be easier therefore to work chronologically, rather than jumping from one period to another. I, I have a list of questions.

CHARLES: What's her name, this someone? Answer me.

SIMON: Susan.

An image of Susan appears on the wall/screen.

SIMON: How did you do that? Where did you get that?

CHARLES: She's twenty-four.

SIMON: I know how old she is. What's she doing up there?

CHARLES: I thought I would paint her, as she is now. Youth is something to be captured, don't you think?

SIMON: Yeah.

CHARLES: I've already begun the preliminary sketches.

SIMON: I don't know what to say.

CHARLES: You're overwhelmed.

SIMON: I am. I'm honoured – well, she will be too. She'll be amazed.

CHARLES: The picture will be yours of course.

SIMON: That's a serious gift – a lot of money. I can't say I understand – you barely know me.

CHARLES: To be young is a wonderful thing. No one knows quite how wonderful until it's over.

SIMON: We have our time I guess.

CHARLES: Yes we do, though some are luckier than others. Time, however, has its price.

The image of Susan now begins to change as an aging process is applied to it.

CHARLES: What do you think of Susan now?

SIMON: I'm not sure. Is this technique something to do with your current work?

CHARLES: Do you still find her attractive?

SIMON: No, not exactly, but if we stayed together then we'd be old together, it wouldn't be this shock.

CHARLES: You wouldn't wish her to be younger?

SIMON: Of course, but what's the point? We get old – it's life. What can we do?

CHARLES: That has been the great theme of my life Simon, of my art. Great paintings live far beyond the lives of their creators, in doing so they ridicule and challenge what we presume to be an inevitable process. They simply don't die.

Light shines through stained glass, getting stronger, thus illustrating Charles' work.

SIMON: But your recent work – the stained glass – is a big move away from the corporeal to the ethereal. Um, would you mind giving my Susan her good looks back, it's a bit disconcerting.

CHARLES: In art of course we can move back in time, like so. (*The image is returned to a youthful one.*) In Science, it's not so easy. But perhaps staying younger longer is possible. Would you desire that Simon?

SIMON: Of course, as long as I had my health, my sanity. I'd like to talk about your work more specifically: the interview.

CHARLES: This is the interview. Oh. You wanted to keep to your list of questions?

SIMON: Just to give some sort of shape.

CHARLES rips them up.

SIMON: But they weren't important, really, just a kind of structure.

CHARLES: When the interview is over you will understand its structure.

SIMON: Oh I see, like the career?

CHARLES: Exactly. And that's how I paint. I never predetermine structure; structure evolves – small discoveries of space and shape. It grows, like a cell that divides again and again until it becomes... what it is.

SIMON: But something, somewhere at the back of your head, is telling you what shape, what colour to select – you are always deciding that one brush stroke is better than another – it's not a random process.

CHARLES: No, but that deep process is still a mystery, that thing that tells us how to evolve – in any direction? Evolution interests me Simon. Should we take hold of it and control it, so that we can predetermine what we become, or just let it run free?

SIMON: I've not really...

CHARLES: Or perhaps you think it would be dangerous to enquire too deeply into what we are and what makes us. Knowing such a thing might destroy us, or at least destroy the function of the artist.

SIMON: Is that why you've never talked about your work before? You're afraid you'll 'lose the muse'?

CHARLES: Desire... is necessary to creation. Purpose, meaning... is necessary to life.

SIMON: So, why have you decided to talk now?

CHARLES: I'm a recluse, as you can see, but eventually everyone has to talk to someone – however dangerous it might be.

SIMON: I can't see how talking to me is a danger to your creative impulse.

CHARLES: The interview is not dangerous for me, Simon.

SIMON: What, for me? Why?

CHARLES: Because nothing will be the same after it. You will learn things, be given knowledge. Knowledge can be dangerous, fatal sometimes. People break under the burden of it. You... are fragile.

Silence. The stained glass light fades.

SIMON: I can't say that I follow one word of that.

CHARLES: I will help you understand. That's why I'm here. In the meantime it's simply that my will to paint, my desire to create, has come to some... conclusion. I seem to have worked in every form, in every colour. I am... waiting... to move on.

SIMON: Right. I think I.... are you telling me – forgive my brevity – that your recent work, the stained glass, is about death, that you have discovered who you are, what makes you, and now you want to die because you no longer have anything to paint about?

CHARLES: Brevity becomes you.

SIMON: And you chose me, to tell the world this?

CHARLES: You chose yourself.

SIMON: Riddle me re.

19

CHARLES: Don't look so worried Simon, I'm not going to kill myself in front of you.

SIMON: Thank you.

CHARLES: Although that day will come, but I still have one thing left to do.

SIMON: What?

CHARLES: Which is to help you.

SIMON: No, you said that day would come. What day? I'm, I'm lost... in this conversation.

Image of Simon's Mother.

CHARLES: Your parents are dead.

SIMON: How did you get this picture? It's in my private album at home.

An image of Simon's Father appears.

CHARLES: Your mother was ten years older than your father – she died of cancer. Your father was struck down with grief and he committed suicide six weeks later. He said he wanted to be with her.

SIMON: How do you know that? And what has my family got to do with this interview? What has this got to with art?

CHARLES: Art is something to do with life, isn't it? Your

father did not want life. He begged God, in whom he did not believe, to let him die.

SIMON: What the fuck has this to do with you? I am not the subject of this interview.

CHARLES: But you are... you are very much the subject of this interview.

Silence. A light. Now we hear a recording of Simon's father's voice.

FATHER: Oh God, let me die, let me die. (*Shouts.*) Simon. Simon.

SIMON: I'm here Father, I'm here.

FATHER: Where is she? Where's your mother?

SIMON: She's... you know where she is.

FATHER: No, I do not know where she is.

SIMON: She's dead. You know she's dead.

FATHER (*breaks down in grief*): Oh God god let me die, let me die.

Silence.

SIMON: How did you record that? What's going on?

CHARLES: I have asked to die – many times. You will ask to die too, you will shout as loud as he.

SIMON: What?

CHARLES: You will beg me to help you die.

SIMON: What the hell are you talking about?

CHARLES: Your Father asked for your help. You refused it.

SIMON: My father was a sick man. He couldn't think straight.

CHARLES: And you must believe that because otherwise it would simply mean that you, his only son, could not give him reason to live.

SIMON: Fuck you.

CHARLES: A reason to live is necessary here. You think he was wrong to commit suicide?

SIMON: Of course he was wrong.

CHARLES: Why?

SIMON: Because life is sacred, arsehole.

CHARLES: Sacred? Are all lives equally sacred? Surely the life of a mass murderer is not as sacred as a man who feeds a starving people? Or are you afraid to judge what is sacred, worthy of worship? Some lives are worthy of such respect, some lives are not. Your life is indeed sacred.

SIMON: What are you talking about? Why have you...?

CHARLES: This is the interview I am willing to give. You see this?

SIMON: Of course I see it.

CHARLES: In this tube, let us imagine, is the cure for your mother's cancer. And I wonder, if you had had this 'magic potion' in your hands, would you have given it to her? Answer the question. Answer!

SIMON: Of course.

CHARLES: Good.

SIMON: Good? What's good?

CHARLES: You would change the so-called natural path of things, of life.

SIMON: To save a life, two lives, of course. So what?

CHARLES: And yet you feel it wrong for your father to do the same thing, take control of his own destiny.

SIMON: My father was a confused man.

CHARLES: As you are Simon. You have the confusions of a good man, the instincts of a good man, to save life if possible, and a natural revulsion against things that, somehow, just feel wrong.

SIMON: The only thing that's wrong is this intrusion into my life. I don't know what game you're playing, but I don't like it and I don't like you.

CHARLES: Well, that's alright, because, you see, I am not a good man. And that concludes our interview.

SIMON: What?

CHARLES: Your confusion must end. I will end it.

SIMON: End it? We haven't talked about your work, your fucking art.

CHARLES: On the contrary, we've talked of nothing else. The interview is over.

SIMON: I can't go back to the office, with this... what? Nothing. (*He holds up his recording equipment.*)

CHARLES: Everything will become clear. Go to the gate.

Light shines. Screen and white wall appears.

CHARLES: You will be shown the way. Go to the gate.

SIMON: But I...

CHARLES: Please.

SIMON (*confused, angry and near tears, he packs up his notes, walks out of the space and onto the screen. There is no gate.*): Well open the bloody gate. (*Under his breath:*) arsehole. Hello? And I want my ID. And my fucking phone. (*He walks as if trying to find the gate, but he walks against a white, unchanging screen.*) Hello? (*He walks back into the space.*) Hello? Charles.

CHARLES appears.

SIMON: I took a wrong turn.

CHARLES: Try again.

SIMON: Try what again?

CHARLES: I told you to leave.

SIMON: You told me to go the gate. I went to the fucking gate and the fucking gate wasn't there.

CHARLES: Try again. Goodbye Simon.

SIMON: ARSEHOLE! (*He walks out of the space and onto the white screen. Still there is no gate. He is now sweating and nervous.*) Shit. Hello, Open the gate. Just flick the switch, just do what has to be done. (*Again he walks against the white screen, then back into the space.*) What are you doing? What is going on?

CHARLES: Tell me what happened?

SIMON: You know very well what happened.

CHARLES: Tell me, make it clear.

SIMON: I couldn't find the gate.

CHARLES: What did you find?

SIMON: Nothing. I just walked and... there's the white wall and I followed it and it leads back here.

CHARLES: But I told you to leave.

SIMON: I tried to leave. What the hell are you doing?

CHARLES: You tried to leave, but?

SIMON: Oh I have to answer? Like in some game show? Is this some fucking game show? Have I been set up?

CHARLES: You tried to leave.

SIMON: Okay okay. I'll play. I tried to leave, but I couldn't.

CHARLES: Because?

SIMON: BECAUSE there was no gate.

CHARLES: There is no gate. There was, but now?

SIMON: You want to talk tenses? You're right about one thing, this interview is over, and I'm going home.

CHARLES: Yes Simon. Go home. Go.

SIMON leaves and in a few moments finds himself back in the space.

SIMON: Open the gate Charles.

CHARLES: If only I could. I've looked and looked but I've never found it. It must move – all the time, be part of some greater wall that surrounds us. It really is a marvellous construction – once inside the wall appears to be... open fields, or mountains, sea, it changes all the time.

SIMON: I want to leave.

CHARLES: I said this wouldn't be easy. I said it was dangerous, that nothing would be the same.

SIMON: Are you telling me that I'm held here, against my will?

CHARLES: I will help you come to terms.

SIMON: For fuck's sake, there is nothing to come to terms with. I came here through a dark space and now I'm going home. Show me the gate! SHOW ME.

CHARLES: I can't, and if could I wouldn't because it would be wrong to let you leave – someone of your importance, someone 'sacred'.

SIMON: What are you saying? No, I don't care, just show me how to leave.

CHARLES: To leave? That would be something – to leave this house, the world, the universe. I desire nothing more. I am a prisoner here too.

SIMON: I am not a prisoner.

CHARLES: Yes, you are.

SIMON: No, this is... this is...

CHARLES: You're afraid?

SIMON: I'm becoming so.

CHARLES: Then go.

SIMON: How can I go, if you can't show me the way?

CHARLES: Precisely, all you can do is accept the new reality.

SIMON: Just help me get out of here. Please.

CHARLES: Simon. You are the first person I've had contact with for many years. Contact with others... was deemed... too risky, scientifically speaking, but you are different.

SIMON: I, I don't understand. Scientifically what?

CHARLES: How can you, but you must understand that it's not me who keeps you here.

SIMON: No one is keeping me here. I'm going back to the office and tonight I'm seeing Susan.

CHARLES: This book is the first book ever published about my work. Of course I had a different name then.

SIMON: I don't give a flying fuck about your work. I never liked it in the first place.

CHARLES: In those days I had a wife and children. They're dead now, all of them.

Image of wife and children – a moving image taken from one of today's video cameras. The fashion of?

CHARLES: That's me in the background. Smiling.

SIMON: What are you saying? Why are you dressed like that?

CHARLES: It was the fashion of the age.

SIMON: That's not possible.

CHARLES: Look at the date the book was published. I was forty when it was published – be careful with it, the binding is not what it used to be.

SIMON: This book is one hundred and sixty years old.

CHARLES: How do I look? The same?

Time passes. Lights rise on SIMON curled up on a bed. CHARLES brings food to the bedside. SIMON hurls it away.

CHARLES: You must eat. You will be kept alive. Whatever else happens you will be kept alive. Simon?

SIMON: If you come near me, I swear to God I'll kill you.

CHARLES: And I would let you do it, but this house will not.

SIMON: GO AWAY.

CHARLES backs away and SIMON weeps.

SIMON: Help me, will someone please... please... please... HELP ME.

Silence.

CHARLES: I will help you Simon.

SIMON leaps from the bed and is about to attack CHARLES. A sound, a light. SIMON loses all strength and collapses at CHARLES' feet. CHARLES wants to help him, but shies away from human contact.

CHARLES: You cannot harm me, or yourself. Simon?

SIMON rolls away.

CHARLES: I've been alone for so long and, strange as it may sound, it is good to see you. The darkness that is in you will fade. Everything will change, in time. When you're ready I will tell you what your purpose is.

Time passes. Darkness. SIMON cries out in the night.

SIMON: Susan, Susan.

CHARLES listens.

SIMON: What have I done? Why am I here? I've done nothing wrong. I'm innocent. Will someone hear me, please? SUSAN.

Time passes. Lights rise. SIMON sits on the end of the bed. Light shines through glass. CHARLES brings a drink to the bedside. After a moment SIMON drinks deeply.

SIMON: You say you are a prisoner too? Who keeps us here? Who built this house?

CHARLES: A mixture of private companies, with government support, and the scientific community who work for both in various ways.

SIMON: And do they – 'they' – have any notion of the complete fucking evilness of this... of this...?

CHARLES: Yes, they do.

SIMON: Do you?

CHARLES: Yes.

SIMON: Then how can you be part of it?

CHARLES: I told you, I'm not a good man nor am I responsible for your incarceration.

SIMON: Then just fucking 'tell' me, in one fucking simple phrase, why am I here?

CHARLES: For the benefit of mankind.

SIMON cries out.

SIMON: What possible benefit can my 'incarceration' have for mankind? What benefit will Susan – a fully paid up, bonafide member of mankind – derive from this 'incarceration'?

I want to see her.

I need to see her. NOW.

CHARLES: It isn't possible. It wouldn't help. She has already begun to rebuild her life.

SIMON: What do you mean?

CHARLES: She can't grieve forever.

SIMON: Grieve, for me? Why?

CHARLES: She will have been given every support, every care will have been taken to help her through. The picture I painted of her will fetch enough money to pay for the rest of her life.

Image of painting of Susan.

SIMON: What are you talking about? What's happened? Oh God, what have they told her? What have they told her?

CHARLES: On your way here, to see me, you had an accident, a terrible accident.

SIMON: They told her... that I'm dead? Oh God. Oh God. No. No. No. (*He collapses.*)

Time passes. Music. CHARLES is working. He takes photos of SIMON asleep. The sleeping position that SIMON is in, should relate to the art work in Act Three. SIMON wakes.

SIMON: How long have I been here?

CHARLES: They let you sleep.

SIMON: For how long?

CHARLES: I don't know, a long time. I don't count anymore.

SIMON: You're insane. The people who built this house are insane, and I will go insane, here with you.

CHARLES: Your only defence is lucidity. Give your thoughts shape – shape is everything. Don't let your thoughts run wild because they are the one thing this house cannot control or possess. Everything else belongs to it. It reads your temperature, your heart rate. It understands what is a happening to your blood, your genes, but it cannot know your mind.

SIMON: Charles, shut up about the stupid house. Someone has told you a lie. Someone, for some reason, has told you that you are nearly two hundred years old. Bollocks, fucking bollocks – no one lives that long. You have lost your mind.

CHARLES: I did, for a time. I didn't have anyone to help me. I was alone here. I'm determined that you will not suffer as I did.

SIMON: Oh, thanks. How kind. But you know, I don't want or need your help, because there is no reason that you can give me – you, who is quite clearly several million light years away from one normal fucking brain cell – can give me that, will make THIS right.

CHARLES: How can you know, until you let me explain?

SIMON: How can you explain anything, that will make any sense? You are deranged, demented, deluded.

Silence.

CHARLES: My sanity is not the question here, it is yours.

SIMON: Great. That's the question? My sanity? I'm kidnapped by a two hundred year old impressionist and you think it's my sanity that's in question. I don't think so. And I don't care.
I just want to go home, or die.
But I forgot, I am dead.
Don't touch me, don't ever fucking touch me.

Silence. SIMON wanders around aimlessly.

SIMON: What is this?

CHARLES: It's a mirror.

SIMON: It has no glass in it.

CHARLES: Then it's not a mirror. Simply the shape of one.

SIMON: It has no function?

CHARLES: I wouldn't say that.

SIMON: What would you say?

CHARLES: I would say... it's art, possibly.

SIMON: How can 'you' not be sure? You the great artist.

CHARLES: Are you hungry? Are you?

SIMON: Yes.

CHARLES: I'll cook.

SIMON: Oh thanks very much, darling.

CHARLES: I like cooking.

SIMON: Oh good, I cook like a bloody student.

CHARLES: Yes I know. (*He pours a drink.*)

CHARLES: A drink?

SIMON: And some peanuts?

CHARLES: You're allergic to peanuts.

SIMON: One fucking peanut, that's all I need. Where the fuck are you going? I thought you were here to help me.

CHARLES (*smiles*): Let me show you round the house.

SIMON: Ah, you're an estate agent. It all becomes clear.

CHARLES: There's a gym. And there's a chapel, I designed myself. There's a pool, a beach, gardens with sunsets and sunrises. There is a life here, Simon.

SIMON: Paradise. I'll be Adam. Unless of course the role's already taken.

CHARLES: And we're not as cut off from the outside world as you might think, but I have found over the years that knowing the problems and conflicts of the world outside, does not bring peace of mind.

SIMON: I will kill myself, I will find a way. Whatever mad experiment is going on here I will kill myself – to spite it.

CHARLES: I thought that you thought life was sacred.

SIMON: Life is. This is not life.

CHARLES: For you no, because you will not allow me to explain the purpose of it.

SIMON: You want to give my life purpose? Don't you think I should be able to give my own life purpose?

CHARLES: You must accept that you're not free. Then your life can begin again. You are not free – and perhaps you never were – even outside these walls. Susan will die, at some time. She is not free to live. You, on the other hand, are not free to die. Shall I continue?

SIMON shrugs. On screen: a chromosome.

CHARLES: What is it?

SIMON: It's obviously you, in your true alien form.

CHARLES: It's a chromosome.

SIMON: Oh no, no, not a... not a chromosome.

CHARLES: A chromosome is...

SIMON: I know what a fucking chromosome is. Why are you showing me this?

CHARLES: Twenty three pairs – one set from each parent – contain all the genetic information that makes us 'us', from the shape of our nose to our ability to catch a ball. Throughout our lives the chromosomes are protected by these tiny telomeres. As we get older the telomeres get shorter, leaving the chromosome open to attack – cells cannot divide properly, they mutate. Once cells do that, we as individuals cannot repair ourselves and we begin to show signs of aging. As the telomeres get shorter still we catch diseases, or grow them inside – cancers, tumours – we begin to die....

SIMON: Yes sir, sorry sir, can I go for a wee sir!

CHARLES: You must understand...

SIMON: I can't sir, I can't, I'm a mere child, an infant, a babe in arms.

Silence.

SIMON: Sorry, do go on and on and on and on.

CHARLES: Perhaps tomorrow.

SIMON: No please, very fascinating: telomeres. Enter Telomeres, stage left. Short little fellow – getting shorter. Please continue.

CHARLES studies him.

SIMON: For fuck's sake, just tell me! What has this to do with me?

Image of a man in his fifties.

CHARLES: How old is this man?

SIMON: Fifty-ish.

CHARLES: Twenty-five.

SIMON: Twenty-five?

Silence.

SIMON: Werner's disease?

CHARLES: Yes. He's aging very rapidly, because his telomeres are getting short very rapidly. You and I, Simon, have the opposite condition. Your telomeres are getting shorter, very slowly. Thus you will age very slowly. In fifty years time, if you have been protected from accident and disease, you will be – appear to be – a young man. You have been given a gift and a curse.

SIMON: This isn't true Charles. Someone is lying.

CHARLES: Those around us will die – we live, as you say, on and on and on and on.

SIMON: And you think that's why we're here? Here.

CHARLES: Yes.

Silence.

SIMON: Okay, fine, let's just say it's true. It's true. We live on and on. (*He laughs at the idea.*) You think that's good?

CHARLES: Doesn't everyone want to live longer? Didn't you want your mother to live? Your father?

SIMON: Fuck you. Trying not to die of cancer and trying to live two hundred years is not the same fucking thing.

CHARLES: And yet they are... intimately connected. Do I not seem healthy, Simon? Look at me. Look! In my eyes alone you will see my age. We are the closest thing to immortal that a human can get. People want what is inside us; our genes, our proteins, our enzymes. We are more valuable to the world than gold, diamonds, plutonium. We are unique, sacred.

Silence.

SIMON: But this isn't true. It isn't true.

CHARLES: You are here because it's true. Do you think they would build a house like this, for just anyone? There are countries that would cost less to buy than this house.

SIMON: Alright, alright. How... how do they experiment upon us, extract what they need? What do they need?

CHARLES: Our DNA, our enzymes, proteins.

SIMON: When?

CHARLES: This house can put us to sleep at any moment – it senses every stress and intercepts any danger. It is... a living cell.

SIMON: So when we're unconscious, these little midgets come in and pull our fucking trousers down? Is that what happens? Or is it machines, like the ones sent to gather rock and dust from Mars? Do little machines come up to us and scrape away at the surface of our skin? (*He giggles madly.*) You don't think, Charles, this is some other kind of experiment?

CHARLES: No.

SIMON: But it could be. A behavioural experiment. For all we know this could be on world TV. Are we on TV, Charles?

CHARLES: No, Simon.

SIMON: But I have this very strong feeling, this isn't real. As if I'm floating, my mind is floating away, into nothing...

CHARLES: This is real. Grasp it, clearly, give it order, shape. All we can do, in our given time in this reality, is behave as well as we can or descend into hell, that is why I'm with you.

SIMON: Oh, ta. You have behaved... impeccably.

CHARLES: One day you'll be free. I believe that. They'll discover the secret. I believe that – and you will live again.

SIMON: But according to you, everyone I ever knew or loved would be dead. (*Yells.*) So what is the fucking point!

CHARLES: Unless, of course, everyone you ever knew or loved were very much alive – because of you.

SIMON: No Charles, this is... it isn't possible.

CHARLES fetches a cage in which there is a live mouse. Silence.

SIMON: What? A fucking mouse?

CHARLES: As long ago as the 1960's scientists identified the enzyme telomeraze as being crucial in the prevention of certain illnesses – such as the cancer that killed your mother – but also crucial to the search for the secret of longer life. This mouse, in human terms, is two hundred and twenty years old. The result of a competition held among scientists, sponsored by business. In mice it is possible to elongate the telomeres by increasing the activity of the enzyme telomeraze in the embryo.

SIMON: But... how... how did I... how did I get this condition? From my parents?

CHARLES: When they discover that, you'll be free.

SIMON: Oh, so, you mean we're the mice?

CHARLES: Yes.

SIMON: Yes. Yes? (*He laughs wildly.*) Okay. That's... that's fun. Let me out, let me fucking out. (*He paces wildly.*)

CHARLES gives him the time.

SIMON: And you... like being a mouse.

CHARLES: Maybe we are the result of some past experiment that has been forgotten, or perhaps we were just an evolutionary accident waiting to happen, for some greater purpose. God's purpose.

SIMON: God? Ah. Not good enough Charles. God died. Didn't they tell you? Went to work one day and just disappeared. He had an accident. A terrible accident.

CHARLES: God is very much alive Simon. God is in you, not abstractly, not metaphorically, but in reality. In your flesh and blood.

SIMON: There is no fucking God, there never was, there never will be. It's a dead idea, a childish fucking notion for primitive people who still think 'potato prints' are great art.

CHARLES: Unless God has changed shape, as everything changes shape. Once, I remember a teacher – a long time ago – who told me that the theory of evolution was the enemy of God, that the whole idea would destroy God. But times moved on as people say, and what if God is, simply, the very process itself? The way the things move from one state to another? God is evolution. And what is evolution? The process of genes mutating to create new species. You and I. You see?

SIMON: Do you know how many times you mentioned God just then? Scary. Oh does that anger you? A little doubt perhaps?

CHARLES: There is no doubt, Simon. The world has changed. It is not the world into which you were born.

SIMON feels the truth of this. Light shines through stained glass.

CHARLES: And If I were to try and paint this God, it would be a balance, a pattern, a shifting light through glass, or water, but it can't be motionless or ever finished because this God is always changing, dividing, inside us, becoming new, but still in this God all the old gods from the beginning of time live on – their hopes of defeating death as fresh as ever.

SIMON: Charles...

CHARLES: Look at the stars Simon, as they die and are reborn. Does the promise of eternal life have no echo in the universe?

SIMON: But you told me that you don't want eternal life, you told me that you wanted to die, that you were waiting to die.

CHARLES: And that is my confusion.

SIMON: Meaning what for pity's sake?

CHARLES: I've played my part. So many years... so many.

SIMON: What are you saying?

CHARLES: To find you was... remarkable. As if someone heard me... crying in the wilderness... and sent you. Surely Simon, I have done enough, to be forgiven, to be excused. To be free.

SIMON: Are you saying that I am... your replacement?

CHARLES: I cannot tell you what I've suffered here.

SIMON: You're telling me that I don't have to be here, that you could continue in this hell, but you were told of my existence and drew me in, so that you could leave. No, no, no, no, no, no. I am not your replacement.

CHARLES: I will help you, I swore that I would.

SIMON: Fuck you, I will not stay here, let me go. Is there any one listening ? Let me go!

CHARLES: You cannot go, you cannot.

SIMON: Then please 'God', let me die, let me die here now.

CHARLES: Simon.

SIMON tries to kill himself by shoving a handkerchief into his throat. Sound, light. He falls into a coma. CHARLES removes the handkerchief. CHARLES then touches SIMON gently on the shoulder.

Act Two

Music. SIMON has created a stage for himself and has dressed in a dinner jacket.

SIMON: I have collected my thoughts.
　　　　I have collected them – in this jar.
　　　　When I drink, my thoughts will take shape.

SIMON drinks. Closes his eyes. Snow falls across him. He opens his eyes, sees the snow. At some stage CHARLES is seen to be watching.

SIMON: I think I was six, we returned to Iceland to see family, but I don't remember the family, what I do remember is standing on a glacier and asking my father why the sea is blue, and my father saying it was to do with how water and light react to each other. He spoke at length, and gave a perfect answer, but still... I was not convinced.

　　　I remember because we stood on the glacier a long time and my feet became so cold that I lost all feeling in them, when they warmed up again I began to cry because it really hurt and my father was ashamed of me crying because of cold feet, he said I was no longer an Icelander. He had this thing about Iceland, its landscapes, its purity, and I felt at some subterranean level that it was my fault he'd had to leave this perfect place, even though I was only an infant when we went to London. So that's what I remember, his chastisement.

　　　He was a tough character – that's what I thought – so it was frightening, odd, to see his complete collapse when my mother died. His soul buckled. His character, unknown to me, was built on thin ice, ice at the edge of the glacier. He drove his car on to a railway track and closed his eyes. He killed sixteen other people – commuters on a high speed train from London. Fate took care of those people as it did the two or three who, on that particular day, just happened to miss the train. Sixteen funerals, and I had letters from some of the families, and they were truly miserable and upsetting because once again, somehow, it was my fault – even if I was powerless to change the course of events, I was to blame. It was in the genes. But then I got to thinking: how dare they blame me. What kind of world would it really be if someone had control over fate – fate is evolution, not God. God is not fate. God is merciful and nothing to do with the random meeting of cells in the primordial past, which then divided and so on and so forth until that day the locomotive left the station – a train of events, so to speak. Out of our control.

I'm on the glacier: 'Mother, why is the sea blue?' 'Because,' she says, 'it wants to be beautiful.' Now that I understood and yet I find myself caught between his notion and hers. Even here I'm torn between them. Who shall I be? Who shall I become here in this... hellish eden? That's not to say that the house is without charm. No, really it's been made by someone who must actually care – about something, even if it's not me.

Are you there? Is anyone there? Is anyone listening?

I have presumed that someone is listening, monitoring my progress in purgatory.

I suppose I would have arrived here many years ago if Mum and Dad had not been liberals opposed to genetic screening, which was standard if not exactly law as it is now, and it's to you I'm speaking, Mother, Father, as well as you, my sweet gaolers.

Because I am here, the reluctant mouse – that's the title of this piece – to make a coherent case against my own existence, because I don't see the need to defeat death. Call me old-fashioned.

And, and, and I'm also trying to understand why exactly I am in this mess because frankly it's confusing, because the care you have taken reveals to me that you know – you must know, in your hearts – that this is wrong. It is sinful and I would urge you to release me back into the world of germs, accidents and misdemeanours which despite its idiocy I was attached to in a degrading sort of way.

Please. Like Now. Pretty Please. (*No answer. Silence.*) It's no bother, I'll try harder. Do better. (*He drinks more thoughts, then closes his eyes. Music – Mozart. He lets the music take him, then opens his eyes.*) That's it I suppose: the big idea. With my genes we could have saved Mozart, Bach, Shakespeare. They could still be living and working. Wolfy composing as Will writes the immortal line, 'To be and to be and to be and to be and to be and to be and to be and to be and to be....' (*The music becomes horribly, painfully discordant – it hurts his ears and he doubles up in pain, cries out in agony. Silence.*) But that does lack a certain grace, a certain shape, and shape is important – stories have their beginnings, middles and ends, reflecting the old reality of our lives, and stories that don't end cannot satisfy the need, the psychological need we have, to know that there is finally a fucking end to every monlogue, including this one.

Even the Bible ends. It just goes on too long for its own fucking good and contradicts itself at every turn, although there are some nice passages. Like the bit about breasts and pomegranates.

You see I'm not unreasonable, and perhaps Will and Wolfy understood the notion of brevity and death itself concentrated their thoughts, spurring them on to produce immortal works.

Through them we have already conquered death.

Haven't we?

Silence, fucking silence.

Life must keep its shape. Its narrative. That's all I'm saying.

But what is shape without meaning?

In art, shape is meaning. In science too. But where's the value?

The Value, if you follow my thoughts, must be in the product because where art and science meet is, is, is, is, is, is in the market place, so perhaps my imprisonment is more commercial than anything else. (*A spotlight shines on a tub of cream.*) Ah, the Simon Gudmundsun anti-aging cream. My picture. (*He opens the tub and rubs cream on his face so that he becomes ghost white.*) How do I look? The same? That's good.

'The enzyme, telomeraze, contained in this non-greasy cream reduces the signs of aging. Say goodbye to wrinkles.'

Goodbye wrinkles.

Sold two million pots a day. There's big money to be made.

But then it might not be corporate at all, it might be criminal.

That's it. I've been kidnapped by arch villains – a dreadful misfortune but a graspable motive. (*Pause.*) But why would criminals put me in a house that costs more than some countries, with walls that change shape and gates that vanish?

No, no, no, criminals would tie me to a chair, poke out my eyes, take my DNA and sell it to the highest bidder. I must be part of some more noble enterprise than that. Someone actually cares, and that's what I'm struggling with – you see... you see... the contradiction. The care and attention to detail.

Then it must be a government initiative – yes, and a

government who had some notion of 'good' would control the product, for the benefit of the world, wouldn't it? And the scientists would tell them what the dangers are. And the danger is that some countries could afford the... the... 'the Gudmundson longevity gene' and those countries would be full of wise old folks and other countries full of stupid young people, made to work like slaves until they attain the freedom, the Roman Citizenship, of old age? They'll be angry, there'll be conflict. Perhaps even war?

But the scientists would foresee the future and come to our rescue. Wouldn't they?

Then come to mine.

If you can hear me, come to mine. (*Silence.*) It's okay, silence is okay, it's my fault, I'll try harder still.

Cos what am I? (*He drinks more thoughts.*) A poor player strutting and fretting my hour upon the stage.

Doctor. Doctor. Doctor.

Calm yourself, Mister Macbeth.

I can't, I can't – my wife is a crown-stealing, king-murdering, hand-washing obsessive and I just don't know why. Oh Doctor.

Don't worry Mister Macbeth, these are natural signs of various genetic predispositions, deep molecular biological arrangements.

Oh, you mean it's not her fault?

Absolutely. For a small fee we can take out the thieving, murderous, obsessive genes and replace them with some new nice ones – soon your wife will be someone else entirely.

Oh that's good, because she was nasty, nasty, nasty.

I understand. You can relax now, relax and don't trouble yourself anymore about why people do things, especially yourself, it's no longer necessary. (*Triumphant music. Light rises on a large model of a double helix.*) From now on everything you need to know is in this perfect little shape. From this day all ambiguity in regard to human action is just vague superficial rambling.

Oh, no more soliloquies?

Absolutely. They were dull anyway. And they no longer have any value because experience can only be given definite meaning by being, how should I say, 'flattened', into this new 'sacred' text, that tells us who we are in a way that is scientifically measurable: the human genome. I call him Helix. You know, for fun. (*He kneels before the helix.*) Helix, my name is Simon Gudmundson, Hi. It's so wonderful to meet you. And you are so good-looking. A perfect shape. A masterpiece. Without you we can't conquer cancer, or death, or anything.

Oh yeah, someone is trying, and you're crucial to the project.

I'm telling the truth.

With you they will not only cure lots of people they can actually stop the diseases occurring again, and we'll all be so much better, we will Helix, we'll be... better people.

That's the promise.

That's the promise.

That's the promise.

Do you mind if I tell you something? Like, confess. Will you be my confessor?

Did you know, Helix, that I was two-timing Susan? I guess you did, I was about to tell her. You know everything, so I am, as you know, a humble piece of shit, but humble me – who has no voice in the vastness of time and space – I have this odd idea that somehow... (*whispers:*) they are WRONG, these businesspeople, government people, scientific people. I know it's, it's heresy, but despite all the benefits I just can't get round to a world where there are no harelips, no... no grief, no death, because there are values implicit in the desire to create the 'proper' shape of a human life, a person without pain or suffering, a post-human, and I feel deep, deep down in my soul that we should respect some of the limitations of our given humanity and, and, and, and, and acknowledge that our limits are inextricably linked with our virtues.

That's it, but... this is the problem: the people keeping me here, they don't think much of my virtues, they don't think much of my soul, they think I'm a mouse.

Do mice have souls? That depends on one's definition of what a soul is. I understand what an arsesoul is, of course – that's them, my gaolers – and mice are not arseholes, they don't imprison people, they are simply mice, and they probably don't have souls, because they can't conceive of having a soul, it would not help their mouseness, but I think, therefore I do have a soul. My soul is that bit of me where my intellect and emotional life meet, to make a third force, a thing beyond molecular biology, beyond the reach of all the clever, clever-clever people.

And it is only now, in this cold palace, that I see their reflection.

I always thought they were more able to judge what was good for me because they understood the details, all the small parts of scientific work which, frankly, would clog up a normal Sunday morning of newspapers and sex, and you see I trusted all the clever-clever people, and now I feel betrayed because I have become part of the detail and that is where the devil lives, he lives here in this loveless place. (*He smashes the double helix to bits.*)

I am not a fucking arrangement of genes.

I am a man.

I want to live, and I want to die.

Because, more than anything else, death defines our

51

humanity because it is a leap in the fucking dark and no one – not a poet, doctor, priest or scientist – can give it shape. It belongs to each of us, alone. It belonged to my father and my mother and I want that, that at least passed down to me. I am their son.

So let me free. Hear me.Will someone please fucking HEAR ME.

Please.

Please.

Please. (*He collapses, exhausted and tearful.*)

Silence. Light rises on CHARLES. CHARLES approaches SIMON, kneels by him and embraces him as if he were a child.

CHARLES (*quietly, but persistent*): Do you think I could have lived here as I do – without purpose? I had a life, once. A wife, children whom I loved. When I became aware of my essential difference and that I could not help them by passing on the miracle that had happened in me, I shut myself away. From a distance I watched them grow old and die.

I could not save her.

I could not save any of them.

I tried to paint – I couldn't. I lost the will to live and yet was condemned to life. But then, with the help of others, those who built this house, I found my true purpose: a noble enterprise.

SIMON: Please stop, Charles. Just hold me.

CHARLES: Shh, I heard you and I will tell you your purpose. The reason for your imprisonment. But you must be prepared to listen. As I have.

Ninety-nine per-cent of all species that ever lived on Earth have become extinct. Why? Because their obsolescence is planned, it's in the genes and we humans must challenge the plan, challenge what you call 'the given', 'our limits', or die out. Death shall have dominion over us. Do you think that is what God wants?

No. God, has revealed Himself to us through science and thrown us a lifeline because the human faces extinction.

SIMON: Charles, Charles, who has told you that the human faces extinction? Whoever told you that has told you a lie. Someone who does not care for you. Someone who wants to use you and sell you and and...

CHARLES: Shh, the extinction lies inside us, in our telomeres.

SIMON: The telomeres. Of course.

CHARLES: Our cells struggle to copy telomeres properly when they divide, and very gradually they become shorter. It's natural, but disastrous because, Simon, shorter telomeres are being passed down and this tiny loss of length from generation to generation will eventually become critical – in the whole species – and then the whole species, everyone, will be open to attack. One powerful bug would be enough to lead to a population crash, a fall of man. But we can save our future, making humans the first species to take hold of our biological destiny, to change what is given and prevent our own extinction. You and I are the hope of all others. That is why you and I are here.

SIMON breaks away.

SIMON: Really? To save the fucking world? Ha ha ha. Do you think I am so in love with myself, so in love with the human race, that I think we have the right to exist eternally? Perhaps we've outlived our time and that is why we are headed for extinction? We are destroying our planet, devouring its every resource, and maybe it's a good thing for some other species that fucked-up humanity disappears.

CHARLES Strikes SIMON a blow that takes SIMON so much by surprise that he is winded and can barely speak.

CHARLES: How tiring you are.

SIMON: You hit me?

CHARLES (*hits him again*): Selfish and mean and programmed to believe hand-me-down ideas. You think death is kind because it's been presented as the only option, but have you really thought about dying, Simon, about your mother as the cancer ate into her bowel?

Why do you think we call death the grim reaper, and not the happy smiley sweeper up? Why do people fear death and fight it to the bitter end? Because it's bad, it's evil. It demands human flesh like some beast, a demon that each day must consume one hundred thousand souls and all their bones and memories are just thrown into its gut and the beast is never full, it simply goes on eating lives, eating experience, and we just let it, but you, Simon, have it in you, in your flesh, to save a hundred thousand lives a day.

And yet if you were free you would chose to condemn them all because of some vague feeling about what is right and wrong. This is beyond right or wrong.

SIMON: Nothing is beyond right or wrong! Nothing.

Image of a child appears.

CHARLES: It is the young who will suffer first – there has never been a generation more open to disease. Their defences are down, and they will pass on this curse to their children.

SIMON: Who is that?

CHARLES: Does it matter?

SIMON: Who is she?

CHARLES: A sick little girl, with no immune system. Do you know her now?

SIMON: No.

CHARLES: You phoned your partner on the day you came here, you had something to tell her, some infidelity. But she had something to tell you, Simon.
    Have you become God yourself, that you would deny your own child the possibility of life? A long, happy life?

SIMON stares at the image of the child which slowly disintegrates and he reaches out to it. Darkness.

Time passes.

Act Three

Music. CHARLES and SIMON dance together – it is funny, sad and gracious, a serious send-up of themselves.

Time passes.

They lay a table for supper with many places.

CHARLES: How does that look?

SIMON: It looks as if we're very popular.

CHARLES: Well, we are. It's your cooking. It's improved, I suppose.

SIMON: Yours hasn't.

CHARLES: No?

SIMON: If anything, it's gone downhill.

CHARLES: Your cooking is definitely on the up.

SIMON: I know.

CHARLES: I've always enjoyed food.

SIMON: But not so much these days.

CHARLES: No, not so much. But, still, food is a miraculous pleasure, always renewed by hunger.

SIMON: Unless one gets too hungry, then it's not pleasurable at all.

CHARLES: Quite. You've put on weight. You look well.

SIMON: Considering.

CHARLES: Yes.

SIMON: I'm not confident though, in your calculations. It feels sometimes that much more time has passed than we think. Sometimes less.

CHARLES: The exact date is available to us.

SIMON: No, we made the right decision.

CHARLES: I think so. Do you like my vegetables?

SIMON: Very nice.

CHARLES: Are they?

SIMON: Of course. You've got green fingers. Old, but green. Experienced. It's a beautiful night.

CHARLES: All nights are beautiful.

SIMON: Why don't you look, then?

CHARLES: It hurts my eyes.

SIMON: Looking at the stars?

CHARLES: Not the stars, simply the act of looking.

SIMON: I want you to look.

CHARLES: Then I shall. Yes, a clear night. Very beautiful.

SIMON: Strange though, to be looking at things which aren't actually there. Just memories.

CHARLES: Yes Simon, I'm aware of the nature of stars.

SIMON: Of course you are. Here's to us and our guests.

They drink.

SIMON: Mm, I dreamt about Susan last night.

CHARLES: I know. I heard you.

SIMON: First time in ages. I dreamt I had children by her – more children.

CHARLES: How touching.

SIMON: Jealous?

CHARLES: Don't be silly.

SIMON: It's not silly. Jealousy is important. Natural.

CHARLES: I'm not jealous.

Silence.

SIMON: I dreamt we made love.

CHARLES: Who?

SIMON: Susan and I. Well, it wasn't love exactly, just good old-fashioned toad in the hole, if you know what I mean.

CHARLES (*indicating the guests*): Must you?

SIMON: Sorry, forgot.

CHARLES: Indeed.

SIMON: But they don't mind.

CHARLES: I think they mind very much.

Silence.

SIMON: No, but it was odd because we had sex then the children just started popping out. There was no pregnancy, just sex and kids. Sixteen of them. And then something terrible happened...

CHARLES: Simon...

SIMON: No, they began to explode – one by one, and only two survived. And there were bits of baby everywhere. It was revolting, but somehow I accepted it because at least there were two left. What do you make of that?

CHARLES: Every new idea is met with revulsion, and every new idea is finally accepted. The revulsion and the acceptance are part of a natural process.

SIMON: I bow to your greater wisdom.

CHARLES: If only.

SIMON: Fuck you.

CHARLES: Must you....

SIMON: Do you really mind? I though that outside of a social context swearing didn't exist.

CHARLES: Our guests.

SIMON: There are no guests, Charles. It's a game, to pass the fucking time.

CHARLES: In any case, two people make a social context.

SIMON: Then obviously my swearing is meant to upset you.

CHARLES: It doesn't upset me, it's simply an annoyance – it makes you sound like a schoolboy. You argue like a schoolboy.

SIMON (*nods*): I think our guests share my basic revulsions. And if you were to ask them here and now, um, for instance if they think it's a good idea to create human beings out of bits of skin, I think they'd all say it was fundamentally a rather bad idea.

CHARLES: Must we go over this again.

SIMON: Again and again and again. Isn't that the joy of it? Answer me! The interview is not over.

CHARLES: If they're right then our guests tonight are the same guests who said the invention of the wheel was unnecessary, that electricity was the work of the devil and that children with incurable diseases should be left out in the cold to die – as nature intended. They can eat elsewhere.

SIMON: Hah- hah- headboy.

CHARLES: You're incorrigible.

SIMON: I've upset you?

CHARLES: No. I'm glad you're incorrigible.

Silence.

SIMON: Our guests seem to be having a nice time.

CHARLES: Yes.

SIMON: When people drink they start to babble, like geese. Can you hear that?

CHARLES: Yes.

SIMON: They're a clever lot though, judging by the range of conversation.

CHARLES: Of course.

SIMON: Of course. We wouldn't invite anyone below par, would we.

CHARLES: I'm a snob, I admit it.

SIMON: I sometimes wonder if I had somehow failed my interview. Your interview. Whichever. I wonder....

CHARLES: I'm tired Simon.

SIMON: I mean, I could have been anyone – someone uneducated, someone with obnoxious opinions, or simply bad personal habits. What would you have done then?

CHARLES: I'd have left you – a long time ago.

SIMON: That's not very nice.

CHARLES: No, but then I'm not human am I.

Silence.

CHARLES: I've been working on something.

SIMON: If it's stained glass I don't want to see it.

CHARLES: No, it's... it's a sculpture, a kind of still life.

SIMON: Really?

CHARLES: Change of form. New beginning. A return. Would you like to see it?

SIMON: If you want me to.

CHARLES: No, I'm asking, would you like to?

SIMON: Of course I'd like to, but only if it's the right time – you know how sensitive you are, when I'm critical.

CHARLES: I'm still vain.

SIMON: And rightly so. Vanity becomes you.

CHARLES moves away.

SIMON: What if I hate it?

CHARLES: What if you love it?

SIMON: I doubt that.

CHARLES: Do you want to see it or not?

SIMON: I was only teasing.

CHARLES: Well don't.

SIMON: Go on then.

A light rises on an art work which is a life study of an eighty year old man with eyes closed, in foetal/sleeping position.

CHARLES: Well?

SIMON: Well what?

CHARLES: What do you think?

SIMON: It's a little old man.

CHARLES: Yes.

SIMON: Is he sleeping or dead?

CHARLES: What do you think?

SIMON: He looks dead. Is it you?

CHARLES: Does it look like me?

SIMON: For God's sake, is it you or not?

CHARLES: I don't know. So, tell me what you think.

SIMON: I think it's fucking upsetting, that's what I think.

CHARLES: But it is rather good, perhaps?

SIMON: Oh Lord yes, it's better than good, it's brilliant. Let's have an opening night – some Chardonnay and some women. Let's all applaud the little dead old man. Guests, guests, gather round.

CHARLES: Don't break it will you.

SIMON: I'd like to.

CHARLES turns away.

SIMON: What?

CHARLES: Nothing.

SIMON: Now you're upset. Charles, dearest, it's a brilliant piece of work, obviously, if anyone could see it, anyone would say the same.
      Are you crying? My God you are, stop it now. It's not you.

CHARLES: This is the third I have made, of these figures.

SIMON: And?

CHARLES: The other two were taken. When I woke they were gone.

SIMON: Has that happened before?

CHARLES: Hundreds of times. I suppose it's a question of storage.

SIMON: Storage? Life really can be very prosaic. You mean that somewhere out there in the real world is a warehouse full of your fucking crap, which they have stolen?

CHARLES: I don't know. Perhaps they sell them – at high prices. I was fetching high prices?

SIMON: Beyond belief.

CHARLES: Such monies could pay for research.

SIMON: And as each piece was taken you felt the impulse to create another?

CHARLES: Yes, it should have been disheartening, but I...

SIMON: It kept you alive, motivated.

CHARLES: Angry. Yes.

SIMON: Then it's for your own good, even though it's essentially wrong.

CHARLES: According to you that isn't possible. This is my last piece.

SIMON: Nonsense.

CHARLES: I don't feel the need to work any more.

SIMON: But you must work, so must I, to keep sane. According to you. I've been writing a great deal. You can read it, read it all.

CHARLES: They don't need me anymore, Simon – they have you. And the research will one day release you.

SIMON: But they never will, because there is no single gene that makes me 'me'.
    Do you hear that? It's a thrush I think.

CHARLES: I made the request.

SIMON: Be quiet, listen.

Bird song.

SIMON: Is that real?

CHARLES: Simon...

SIMON: Shut up!

Bird song fades.

SIMON: How did you request permission?

CHARLES: You speak, they answer.

SIMON: I've tried that – a thousand times. No one answers.

CHARLES: When I leave, they will answer. They will speak to you every day, as much as you like. There's a format.

SIMON: But it doesn't matter. You're not going.

CHARLES: It's time...

SIMON: Time?

CHARLES: I requested permission.

SIMON: It doesn't matter, they won't let you go. They won't. Don't you remember, you have these strange mutant genes which enable you to live on and on and they need you here – you are the centre of their 'research', and there are still so many people you can assist, who suffer and die, all because their telomeres aren't like yours, and how can you after all this time just run out on these people? You have what they want and you are just going to commit suicide. That's what it is. And that contradicts everything.

You can't leave me here alone.

It would simply be wrong. There is such a thing.

Don't go. Please.

I'll... I'll stop swearing. (*He laughs.*) I'll do anything...

CHARLES: Simon...

SIMON: I won't let you go.

CHARLES: I've already stayed much longer than I thought, because...

SIMON: Because we're not meant to be alone. Death is being alone, isn't it?

I don't know what it is, but you're not ready, you can't be, look at you – so full of life, still.

Don't go, Charles. Please. Please.

Hear my prayer. You at least can do that .

Silence.

CHARLES: I'll wait.

SIMON: I'd prefer you to stay, rather than wait. Without you, I would perish.

CHARLES: I'll stay.

SIMON: For me?

CHARLES: Yes Simon.

SIMON: I'm not strong like you, Charles.

CHARLES: You're stronger than you think.

SIMON: One day. Charles. we'll both be released, when they discover the secret, they will let us go, and your work will... it will... flourish again.

CHARLES: Thank you, Simon.

SIMON hugs CHARLES. CHARLES allows the contact.

CHARLES: We should eat. The table's ready.

SIMON: What about him?

CHARLES: He's not hungry.

They smile. They sit down to eat. Lights fade. A sound. SIMON falls asleep.

Music. The gate, the dark space in the white wall, appears and the mirror is aligned to it. CHARLES, after touching SIMON once upon his head, slowly walks through the mirror itself and disappears.

Time passes. SIMON wakes. He is at the table. The still life/sculpture has gone.

SIMON: Charles? Charles! CHARLES.

The neon Frame of the MIRROR slowly becomes light. SIMON approaches it.

SIMON: Are you there? Is someone there?

MIRROR: Yes, Simon.

SIMON: Who are you?

MIRROR: We are a non-profit research foundation sponsored by corporations and government agencies. We are dedicated to truly fulfilling the dream of healthy, radical, life extension.

SIMON: Why am I here?

MIRROR: For the benefit of mankind.

All other light fades.

The End.

The Company

Malcolm James (Charles)
Theatre includes: *Mrs Warren's Profession* (Bristol Old Vic); *The Lady In The Van*, *The Tempest* and *The Nutcracker* (West Yorkshire Playhouse); *Old King Cole* (Cochrane Theatre, London); *Kes*, *Romeo and Juliet*, *Ham*, *Toad of Toad Hall*, *Second From Last In the Sack Race*, *Neville's Island* and *Travels With My Aunt* (New Vic, Stoke-On-Trent); *Sleeping Beauty* (Theatre Royal, Northampton); *King Lear* (Sheffield Crucible); *My Sister In This House* (Theatr Clwyd); *My Night With Reg* (Library Theatre, Manchester); *Rosencrantz and Guildenstern are Dead* and *Volpone* (National Theatre); *Much Ado About Nothing*, *A Midsummer Night's Dream* and *The Merry Wives Of Windsor* (Regent's Park Open Air Theatre). Television and Film includes: *Brookside*; *Crossroads*; *The Bill*; *Tales From The Tower*; *The Roman Tragedies*. Radio includes: Will Self's *Letters To An Icon*; *The History Man*.

Danny Nutt (Simon)
Danny trained at Rose Bruford College of Speech and Drama. Theatre includes: *The Lion, The Witch and The Wardrobe*, *To Kill A Mockingbird* and *Master Harold and The Boys* (Leicester Haymarket); *The Rivals* (Compass Theatre); *Bad Blood* (Theatre Royal, Windsor and tour); *Romeo & Juliet* (Creation Theatre); *Equus* (Salisbury Playhouse); *House/Garden*, *Knights in Plastic Armour* and *Body Language* (Stephen Joseph Theatre and tour all directed by Alan Ayckbourn); *Lord of The Flies* (Lyric, Hammersmith and tour); *The Pirates of Penzance* (West Yorkshire Playhouse); *Oliver!*, *October's Children*, *Captain Stirrick*, *The Ragged Child* and *Aesop* (National Youth Music Theatre). Television includes: *Doctors*, *Keen Eddie*, *Footballers' Wives*, *The Bill*, *Casualty*, *The Infinite Worlds of H.G. Wells*, *Danger Field*, *The Age Thing*, *London's Burning*, *Family Affairs* and *I'm Alan Partridge*. Film includes: *Luminal*, *The Trench* and *Velvet Goldmine*.

Kate Saxon (Director)
Directing credits include: *Nine Parts of Desire* (Public Theatre, NY, USA); *Humble Boy* (Northcott Theatre, Exeter); *Trust Byron* (The Gate and tour); *The French Lieutenant's Woman* (Fulton Opera House, USA); *The Secret Garden* (Salisbury Playhouse); *Scratching The Façade* (Birmingham Rep and Symphony Hall); *Shelter* (Palace Theatre, Watford); *Grimm Tales*, *The Little Prince* (ATY, Alaska), *adrenalin...heart* (Arcola) and Associate Director, *After Mrs Rochester*, for Shared Experience (West End and International Tour). Kate has developed new writing and directed rehearsed readings and projects for The Royal Court, The Bush, Soho Theatre, and The Arts. In Opera, Kate has directed *la Bohème* (revival, Opera North), and assisted at Garsington, Bregenz Festival Opera, Austria and Opera North. Kate produced *Captain of the Birds* for Abacus Arts at The Young Vic. Kate is Associate Director for Shared Experience Theatre Company.

Alex Eales (Designer)
Alex trained at Wimbledon School of Art. Previous designs include: *The Country* (Belgrade Theatre); *Serious Money* (Cambridge Arts Theatre); *Girls Night* (National Tour); *Girls Behind* and *Tractor Girls* (National Tour). He was Costume Designer for *Iron* (Traverse, Royal Court Theatre Downstairs and Leipzig Shauspeil, Germany). He also designed *The Suicide* for Teatro della Contradizione, Milan. He was Design Associate on the 2005 production of *A Dream Play* (RNT) and was Resident Designer for E15 Acting School during 2000. He also teaches part-time at Wimbledon School of Art. He has designed over sixty shows in the last seven years and assisted on designs for the Royal National Theatre, ENO, Glyndebourne Festival Opera, among others.

Bruno Poet (Lighting Designer)
Bruno has lit over 100 productions of theatre, opera and dance in the UK and Europe. Over the past year his work has ranged from Theatre shows in London (*Dumb Show* at the Royal Court, *Don Juan* at the Hammersmith Lyric), Manchester (*Volpone* at the Royal Exchange), Bristol (*Alice In Wonderland* for the Old Vic Theatre) and Leeds (*The Lemon Princess* for the Caird Company at the West Yorkshire Playhouse) to his seventh consecutive season for Garsington Opera and Operas in Bologna, Italy (*Leonore*) and Antwerp, Belgium (*Arabella*).

Thomas Hall (Video Designer)
Thomas is an artist and filmmaker. Artistically, he is interested in public intervention and empowerment with media technology. His artwork has toured nationally and internationally and uses new technologies (such as motion tracking and image matting) and large-scale projection sited within public spaces. His short films and music videos have been shown at numerous festivals and broadcast on national networks. Recent moving image projects for theatre have included *The Lion, The Witch and The Wardrobe* and *Captured Live*, for Leiecster Haymarket Theatre. Future projects include music videos for Deep Water Recordings and a large public piece for the market square in Nottingham.

Richard Price (Sound Designer)
Richard completed several successful rock and roll tours up and down the country after University. From here he went on to the MAC in Birmingham and later onto the Belgrade Theatre in Coventry. Theatre includes: *Leader Of The Pack*, *Good Companions*, *Limestone Cowboy*, *3 Minute Heroes*, *The Wedding* and several pantomimes (The Belgrade); *The Crucible*, *East Is East*, *The Wizard Of Oz*, *Peter Pan*, *A Little Night Music* and *Unsuitable Girls* (Leicester Haymarket Theatre). In 2002 and 2003 Richard designed and operated the sound for

Mardi Gras and *Solid Gold* at the Ibiza Marquee. In 2003 Richard was appointed as Head of Sound at the Theatre Royal Plymouth. Recent credits include Sound Designer on *Dick Whittington* and *Yeoman Of The Guard*.

Alexander Ferris (Assistant Director)
Alexander is a young director with a passion for new writing. Since graduating from Liverpool John Moore's University in 2001, his directing credits include: *Cuckoo* (Sherman Youth Theatre); *Meat* by Owen Thomas (nominated for a Theatre in Wales award); *L'Hotel* (Jarbones Theatre Company). He has also directed numerous rehearsed readings for UnZipped at the Sherman Theatre, Cardiff. As an assistant director he has worked on Sgript Cymru's production of *Crossings* by Clare Duffy and Made in Wales's production of *Football* by Lewis Davies.

Rebecca Gould (Producer)
Rebecca is Associate Director at the Theatre Royal and an Education Associate at the National Theatre. She has recently produced *Football* by Lewis Davies for Made in Wales at the Edinburgh Festival. Directing work includes: *The Wonderful Life and Miserable Death of the Renowned Magician Doctor Faustus* and *Little Tempest* (National Theatre); *Romeo and Juliet* (English Shakespeare Company); *Venus* by Peter Morgan and *Gulp* by Roger Williams (Made in Wales); *The Jolly Folly of Polly the Scottish Trolley Dolly* and *Eggplant* by Greg Ashton and James Williams for The International Festival of Lilliput.

Theatre Royal Plymouth

The Theatre Royal Plymouth is one of the most successful regional producing and touring lyric theatres in the UK. The organisation consists of two, distinctive performance spaces: the Theatre Royal and the Drum Theatre, as well as TR2 – an award-winning theatre production and education centre.

The range of work presented and produced at the Theatre Royal is vast, making it one of the best attended regional producing theatres. National companies that make the Theatre Royal their home in the South West include Birmingham Royal Ballet, Glyndebourne, Welsh National Opera, and Rambert. In addition, we welcome major touring drama, musical and dance productions.

The Theatre Royal also produces or co-produces a number of drama and musical productions each year, many of which transfer to the West End or tour nationally. As part of an ongoing collaboration with the producer Thelma Holt, the Theatre Royal has also produced a series of Shakespeare productions which have been successful on national tour.

However, the Theatre Royal is only one auditorium. The Drum Theatre is a smaller, new-writing venue that welcomes and produces the most innovative and cutting edge new work in the UK. An exceptional venue in the South West, the Drum enjoys a national reputation for the highest quality, and as one of the most exciting centres for new writing, regularly producing with Frantic Assembly, The Bush, Paines Plough, Royal Court, Told By An Idiot, and Out of Joint.

The newest addition to the organisation is TR2 – our production and education centre. A truly unique facility in the UK, this state-of-the-art, award-winning building provides unrivalled production, wardrobe and rehearsal facilities which enable the theatre to continually produce work for both stages. But production is only one part of its existence. At TR2, the Arts Development and Education team provide an essential service to the local and regional community. As well as running youth and community theatre groups, the team also works with educational establishments throughout the South West on projects ranging from skills-based workshops to large-scale performance projects. The capacity of TR2 enables the theatre to run one of the biggest education and outreach programmes in a regional venue in the UK, and our objective is to continue to expand and develop this work.

The Theatre Royal Plymouth is a forward thinking and creative organisation which aims to be a cultural resource for its local community, the wider South West region, and for a national audience.